SAID NOT SAID

Also by Fred Marchant

Poetry
Tipping Point
Full Moon Boat
House on Water, House in Air
The Looking House

Translation
From a Corner of My Yard by Trần Dăng Khoa
    (Co-translated with Nguyễn Bá Chung)
Côn Đảo Prison Songs by Võ Quê
    (Co-translated with Nguyễn Bá Chung)

Editor
Another World Instead: The Early Poems of William Stafford, 1937–1947

SAID NOT SAID

poems | Fred Marchant

Graywolf Press

This publication is made possible, in part, by the voters of Minnesota through a
Minnesota State Arts Board Operating Support grant, thanks to a legislative appro-
priation from the arts and cultural heritage fund, and a grant from the Wells Fargo
Foundation. Significant support has also been provided by Target, the McKnight
Foundation, the Amazon Literary Partnership, and other generous contributions from
foundations, corporations, and individuals. To these organizations and individuals
we offer our heartfelt thanks.

Published by Graywolf Press
250 Third Avenue North, Suite 600
Minneapolis, Minnesota 55401

www.graywolfpress.org

Published in the United States of America

ISBN 978-1-55597-773-3

2 4 6 8 9 7 5 3 1
First Graywolf Printing, 2017

Library of Congress Control Number: 2016951420

Cover design: Kyle G. Hunter

Cover art: Peter Sacks, from the *Codex* series. Courtesy of the Marlborough Gallery.

for Stefi

&

James Carroll

Contents

Use your head, can't you, use your head, you're on earth, there's no cure for that!
Samuel Beckett

ONE

Psalm

So why bother with it, let it go,
      this business of deciding if,
or how long, a string of words
      should take to stretch across
a page, or float, as if weightless,
      or reach down like a priest
who after listening to your list
      says you are forgiven. This is
not something for a grown-up
      to worry about, nor is it for
anyone who votes, or is listed
      demurely as *head of household*.
Nor is it your question for today,
      not after you have, in traffic,
followed a purple flag to
      a grave where inches down
in East Providence, RI,
      a yellow backhoe has revealed
a layer of vivid red clay.
      The workmen who loop the straps
under the coffin are whispering,
      wondering if the seal remains true.
In this question they are like
      the priest who, upon finishing
his *Prayer for the Dead*, offers
      remarks on *the poet* by which
he means the psalmist, that singer
      who, though he knows better,
insists: *when I call, answer me, God.*

The Unacceptable

How?

How *do* you write about a cough?

How to hint at the sound of it?

A cough that was *odd*, not from a cold, or something else you catch.

I think now it was the sound of what was eating away my sister's mind.

I first heard it at our grandfather's funeral Mass.

I was seven and thought she should just *quit it*, stop bothering me, and everyone.

Forty Years

Howard, her life spent on William A. Howard's farm, *Howard* the short form for what was originally the Asylum for the Incurable Insane.

How the gentle Pawtuxet stream flowed past, and how I composed a song she could sing under her blanket:

O bless this sweet layer of wool, bless my warm halo of heat.

How the illness clutched her by the neck, tossed her up and let her go, and in the second before she landed, how she thought she might escape, could drift away like smoke from a long drag on her cork-tipped Kool.

How the sound of the rust-bucket trawler named *Memory* followed her wherever she went, its iron nets dragged across the floor of her being, the silt clouds and debris fields, a stern winch sounding a lot like pain.

How she ached to have them examine what they pulled up there, some of it thrown back, some saved in the ice-hold: a few scaled creatures to be studied in the labs, their weird antediluvian appendages, their would-be limbs.

How rage at times so transformed her face I was sure she and Nero had gone fishing in the lake of darkness, and me, I had become the sane but cleverly gibbering Edgar hiding in the hollow of a tree.

Howard, a downbeat, and off beat, a first note in the music we heard when the kitchen knife found its home in her hand as she reached in the drawer.

How the legal involuntary moved in and imposed itself because the great orange snowplows out on the mid-winter highway were trying to run her down.

Me

To her I was airy sunlit ice, a comet tail, in an elliptical once-in-a-while orbit, a vague portent, a streaky omen, with nothing much to say anymore, just the rest of my self-comforting ditty.

Bless the blanket over her head and under her feet.
Bless the hands that weave the thread.
Bless the sheep they sheared it from.

Our father, meaning to protect me, said it would be good for me to visit and *see this*, so I'd know, so I would *know know know* how not to end up here or there or wherever Howard actually was or would in my life someday be.

I too wanted to give that place and her a world of berth, the Xmas visits all I ever had to do really, just get a box with stick-on ribbon, some CVS shampoo, wrap it in paper printed with holly, candles, Victorian joy.

An hour in the Howard parking lot, my father and I signing her out to the backseat where she opened what we brought her, a chocolate interlude, an engine idling, the heat on.

Our spot outside her own red brick *How* and her wherefore *Ward*, decked out year after year in the tinsel and the garlands of disordered thought.

Howard, our one and only name for the world headquarters, the genuine article, real deal *skit-so-free-nee-ya*, its live-in campus to the left of the cornfields, just off Rte. 2, heading south from Providence.

Her

Her last day on the planet she thrashed and spit while the nurses tied her wrists to the bedrail with strips of cloth that only worsened what was happening.

Her face was radiant, her whole being flush from the long struggle with those she knew she should never have trusted.

They tried to keep track of her vitals, charted her erratic heart, peered into her cranium with a flashlight through the eyes.

She said they had taped a death-line to the port in her arm.

They said she should believe in the plastic tube at her nose, that it would fill her lungs with good clean air.

She shook her head as hard as she could, got her whole body to say nope, *thou shalt not*, no way, nothing doing, *thou shalt not touch me*.

Not with the elbow-bendable straw adjusted to the lips, not with the insidious needle pointed upward and dribbling over.

And absolutely not with that wheezing apparatus of the unacceptable the big attendant in his scrubs was wheeling in.

In the As If

we plan to stuff steel wool down the doctor's throat get lighter fluid

ronson

squirt it in his ears and up his hairy nose ignite that fucker inside out

my-my-myelin

while an infinitely dull month passes between first pills and the pucker

tardive

and lip-smack on the day after the tomorrow when your head starts to

trigger

nod like a horse trained to say yes the tongue feeling a little loblolly

semiotic

and pink as a dog's a tongue that says you're late for the prom you're

sorry

so sorry until one morning a pinto-splotched nerve gallops into the corral

bushwhacked

where your old inner wrangler straddles the fence a lasso and snaffle

paladin

draped over his arm while his fingers scratch the pony behind the ear

jangling

as good cowboys do while telling the bewildered animal all will be

¡hola!

well in all the ways nerves have when they start to nicker and twitch

okeydokey

while the stray dogie-tongue rearranges a chaw I must never never

spit

Intake Retake

A hand reaches out to help you across
       you feel the swell under a shifting point

of contact and hear the ropes strain as if
       you are a boat entering the harbor passing

a red outer buoy where the gulls perch
       watching and waiting for you to tie up

shut down the twin engines and stare
       into a waxy Dixie cup the diameter of

a silver dollar and in which two major
       tranquilizers float on a rising tide while

on the dock gather those who want to hear
       the tasty details in your story's close calls

with love and the lazy firing pins unwilling
       as ever to cooperate and relieve you of duty

ok I'm back now is what you say to ruddy
       non-responders on whom nothing is lost

or past or forgotten especially getaways
       like yours so you toss the thick manila

folder of your history to a longshoreman
       whose beefy nonchalance you say reminds

you of dinghies on the *Titanic* yes but not
        a good association given the expert coming

in under a crushed hat with pheasant feather
        angling 45 degrees up from the cerebellum

as if his jowly being was a taxi whose sign
        is lit and says he is on duty though you are not

sure what he says or if he has asked a question
        but you have dis-remembered more many times

before so you say the best words you own
        for his parsing by which you intend to show

him you are truly *compos* in search of a verb
        and its subject and only then do you go out

on a limb for the complement which as you
        say to anyone within the sound of your voice

is spelled with an e and means the sentence
        and these thoughts hereby are now over.

Cement Mixer

I helped her board the windows,
                    spit in the dresser, shut the gate.
She was the legatee,
                    a *this is this* tattoo on her arm,
glazed roads to look down,
                    glimpses of a sky-burial.

Mournful pines, a girl's wandering mind.

There was always ragweed
                    and burdock to welcome her back,
hints of love and friendly
                    lower organisms—moss, algae.
She was soaked to the skin with tears
                    she had yet to shed.

Then it was back out to sea, a ferry taking on water.

She lived out the rest of her stints
                    beyond the idea of salvation,
with four to a room, a stand-up
                    tub to shower in, shallow sink,
the remnant of an easy chair,
                    long gleaming linoleum halls.

Gummy flowers pasted on the wired door.

Asylum, refuge, sanctuary
                red-brick palace of peeling paint,
oaks brushing against the walls,
                her group sing in the every a.m.,
a gray-haired volunteer at the piano,
                the rows of folding metal chairs.

Slim Gaillard to get the day going right.

Cement mixer, put-ti, put-ti,
                cement mixer, put-ti, put-ti,
a little poodle da skoodie,
        and poodle da skoodie some more,
that is how, that sure is how,
                you make the good concrete.

twin	**tulips**
I ran	a finger
down her	stilt-like
stems and	over pale
green petals	my sister's
watercolor	the paint
weeping	down the
page she	was trying
to hold	onto as
long as	as long as

The Name of the Painting

on Titian's Europa (The Rape of Europa)

In her exposition the docent avoids the word *rape*,
as does the museum in the brass nameplate beneath.

She says the work is a literal tornado of unfinished
diagonals in an unfinished story, thus violating all

boundaries of time and frame, inventing the modern.
A pair of putti with arrows hover over the woman

while another cherub rides on a green scaly fish
and stares up Europa's loosened skirt. Her sisters

on the dim shores of Sidon are waving in dismay.
In the distance they are so tiny you can barely find them.

What you do see clearly is how tightly she grips
the chalky horn of the bull, while over her head flows

the wild red scarf that Ovid mentions. The docent
says the energy of that swirl hints at ambivalence

and the lure of an adventure, noting in an aside
that the word *rape* is kin to rapture, the scarf like

a wild force lifting her up. The girl's face, however,
is filled with palpable fear, her brow pale as the far,

private reaches of her thigh. The putti, the lewd fish,
and we standing in the gallery all eye her nakedness

at the center of the painting. Some say the bull too
peers with desire over the folds of muscle in its neck,

but the animal looks as frightened as the girl he carries,
and senses some lascivious and indifferent Almighty

intending mayhem has taken over its body. Plus,
there is this screaming creature flailing on its back.

At first the bull had let her lean on its flank, touch
like a feather, but when the command or urge came on,

the animal was compelled to turn with all its strength
toward the western sea. The instant it happens the girl

knows this is forever. As she looks back at the life she
is leaving, her eyes turning into dots of terror, I realize

I am seeing my sister again, how her madness descended
or rose up beneath her, took her beyond known islands,

washed her up in a geri-chair, delivered her to the shore
of a bright-lit dayroom where the whiteboard waited for

a nurse with a thick magic marker to fill in the blank
Today Is

TWO

A Bone in the Throat

Imagine a fishbone lodged in your throat.
Imagine it kicks and squirms.
You cough, you hack, you try to heave it out.

As you are human, you adapt,
you learn how to speak, eat, sleep, work,
and dream with this thing within.

You read the stories of tumors like grapefruits.
There is nothing consoling in reports
of massive and painful deformity worldwide.

Imagine your children inherit the problem,
though you know the issue is not genetic.
Periodically there is violent physical reaction,

a rejection, but nothing changes.
In the early hours just after your prayer,
and before splashes of water clear the eyes,

you try as you may to discern meaning
in the situation. You feel the bone stirring again.
It is like a dog you have awakened.

You do not marvel anymore at metamorphoses
such as that from cyst into a cancer,
the tumor that turns into a dog.

Suddenly, the whole neighborhood is barking.
Trials and dangers await you. The racket
makes you run to your child's bedside.

Now what do you do?

The window is wide open.

For some indecipherable reason, she has stopped breathing.

Here is what the mind does

when my laptop opens to a small red car
a tight street in Jenin gray-yellow dust
an electric window half-open and five
lean-to cards where on each a number
denotes a round spent or the place where
it began to travel at the speed of its idea
while by an open car door the blood pools
pools and follows a tilt in the road—not
far—more a lingering as if blood could
choose not to leave could hang around
be curious and puzzled like the children
who stop to watch men who have duties
do them as quickly as they can in a slow
reluctant and deliberate picking through
which is what the mind does at moments
like this—really little more than nothing

From The Sender

Pupils, jittering eyelids, axons,
random charges, scribbled nerves,
images arrayed like iron filings,
our magnetic north, the dog star,
rotating spits, an arc of language,
an impatient dream clamoring at
the door like a small wet animal
barely alive, who looks up as if
to say *The Sender* wants you to
do more *deliberate reasoning*,
knock off the cascading syntax,
quit acting like a puppy in a pool.

Consider then the captured dictator,
his bound arms, sweat-matted hair,
and his dark, bewildered little eyes.
Listen to the inaudible plea he makes
for mercy, though he knows full well
there will be none, not today, not in
the desert light that gives to his body
the soft glow of sacrifice, not with his
face chiseled like a goat's whose neck
is held open to the knife, whose legs
and hooves start to twitch, just now
remembering they are supposed to run.

Marwan,

who says the only work left
is to read the olive trees,

      takes me to his groves,

who stays awake all night while
I sleep on his foam pads,

      a sweater hooding my eyes,

who taps the plastic keys,
works the Translate screen,

      his sole companion,

who greets me when I wake,
says he is not sheep, not goat.

      What he means is the قسوة

is a wind that scorches the air,
makes it impossible to breathe,

      let alone translate.

Below the Fold

someone in Benghazi with a hose in one hand
uses his free one to wipe down the corpse
water flows over the body and down
a tilted steel tray toward the drain

                                        what washes off washes off

E pluribus animus

One-soul sits weeping on the seawall,
a hero wishing to flee the enchantment.

Dog-soul stands guard, swivel-headed,
guarding its bony idea of the enemy.

Good-finger-soul twitches as it labors
to keep the chamber oiled and clean.

Soothe-soul wipes with a gauzy swath,
circles of comfort on the blued metal.

Prickly-wire-brush-soul scrubs the lands
and grooves free of the flecks of the past.

Hand-soul weighs the weapon, marvels
at its simplicity, service, and perfect fit.

King Chestnut

Earthworm, seedpod, the hidden life
      inside the sable skin of horse-chestnuts,

the tree-grounds littered with them,
      each perfect to drill a hole through,

hang at the end of a rawhide strand.
      We had no name for the game that

had you hold your arm out straight,
      steadying the chestnut dangling under,

while another boy took aim with his
      and tried to smash yours to pieces.

The best you kept in the cigar-box
      papered with gilded royal faces,

fit company, along with the screws
      and washers, for a king chestnut

growing aged, wrinkled, and hard,
      what you hoped for, getting ready.

Quitter's Rose

The San Diego recruit depot unit signs
in gold lettering, city airport next door,
a smiling Nanook painted on the tailfin
watching over ropes that dangled from
the O course, its obstacles empty now,
but as I leaned into the plane's window
I saw my young self shinnying up, trying
to touch a creosote crossbeam at the top.
A callus ripped open under my fingers,
the palm a mess of blood, skin, rope-hair.
Just shy of the top I let go not knowing
how much this was a failure of character,
but when I landed unhurt in the sawdust
I felt giddy with relief, as if I had come
back alive, maybe even won a medal.

Quảng Tri Elegy

I am pretty sure that I would have died here,
maybe in the rain that comes down to pick
at the old, red-clay road snaking upward;
I am pretty sure I would have killed here,
or wanted to, had to, tried to, not meant to,
with no god, and few others to forgive me.

—

I bow over the gravestones, and the burning
sticks bow with me, my spine, all my pliable
inner organs bowing with a sorrow I barely
know I have, but which a honeyed, musky
joss calls out of me, a smoke-dragon rising
before which all I am bows, then bows again.

—

On the road into the mountains, mist clings
to the trees, wraps its arms around the rows
of gravestones. I ask what nights were like,
what lights shone in the valleys, what smoke
rose from cooking fires, what whispers you
listened for in words you did not understand.

—

At Khe Sanh, in the small museum on stilts,
glass cases keep the rifles, packs, jungle boots.
On the walls many framed photos of the siege.
Beside me a friend from Hanoi leans in to find
himself in the pictures, searching as in the koan
for the face he had before his parents were born.

—

On the bus ride back down from Lao Bảo,
I see children playing in a corner of the yard,
and wonder if they have heard the story of
the dead who come down to the river at night
to bathe, who edge out on the mossy rocks,
and let the fast water wash over what they are.

—

It is said they listen to crickets sing, the wind
murmur, a listening as deep and real as breathing.
They scrub their hands, they splash their cheeks
and steady each other in the water, these shades
the stream rushes toward, eager to give them
back their flesh unharmed, their mothers' own.

The Peach

by Võ Quê

co-translated with Nguyễn Bá Chung

Overnight, a bat has eaten half the peach,
    the rest has fallen onto the sad, sad earth.

For you, I leave a portion of happiness.
    Me, I shall keep my share of the sorrow.

Crossing Nguyễn Du Street

Hà Nội

Advice we had was to just step right out,
    like wading

in a stream. Motorbikes—hundreds of them—
    would find

a way around us. We must not be hesitant,
    for that

would throw everyone off. So, trusting these
    our friends

here on the street named for the poet of *Kiều*,
    we leaned

into the traffic as if it were only a light wind
    flowing round

our faces. At that instant I tried to imagine
    a world

completely merciful, and belonging to those
    few who,

as they passed smiling, looked as if they just
    might forgive us.

Trip Wire Dream

the night fell like the snow that had been falling all day

unlike

a peach pit as wet and red as the cancer they've removed

like

the tyrant untethered from his broken clean-shaven neck

unlike

the battalion of army ants crossing over his deserted lips

like

an unfathomable prayer on the overseas shortwave radio

unlike

the role that curses played in my earliest mature verses

like

a day beginning with the snow that was falling all night

unlike

Passage Tomb

DayGlo brands on the sheep, barbed gates we barely slip through,
green pasture mound, the afterthought rubble where we peer in, eyes
adjusting to stones shaped like the lives it took to heft granite to canopy.

I'd pry the whole thing apart, brush away the dirt, peel mica from quartz
find the flecks of light, and ask how deep the vein goes, this desire to work
ore to metal down to blade, run a thumb along the edge, and say *not bad.*

I imagine bends in the passage, dust-puffs under our feet, a few places
where water seeps in from the pasture above, a dank air that rushes toward
us and pushes back, none of it with anything more to say about the matter.

Checkpoint

you are cooperative

you are educated

sing arias at home

you nod meaning

yes and lift up your

shirt to show the

center of your torso

is as hairless and

innocent as the day

you were born

which of course you

do not remember

but at this point

the air and warm

light that touches

your inspected and

guaranteed to be

unthreatening flesh

turns you into an

infant who is glad

the mother from

whose stomach he

sprang is no longer

among the living

and cannot witness

or ease his shame.

Ghost Ranch

Slits in nothingness are not very easy to paint.
—Georgia O'Keeffe

Ram's Head
a horn curved like a petal
layered into a flute,
the bone made to sing
what is hiding in the hollows.

Hollyhock
my friend says
a poem is a column of air,
or a sorrow-flower,
a yellow-white star.

Little Hills
the brown earth listens
to what the red earth says,
angry clouds gather
like the Lord's left hand.

Night Sun
after the killing
a searchlight
the color of bone
to sweep us clean.

THREE

Two Minutes

Some thoughts teem as if in a vernal pool,
peepers throbbing on the waters below.

—

The gaudy monarch-thoughts migrate on
a raft of their own dead, save for the few.

Wod-or

Indo-European root for water

pollution

14th century: related to the discharge of semen other than during sex, as in playing with yourself or the wet dreams you had while sleeping in the corner of your sibling's bed, or was it during one of those periodic possessions that sometimes overtake you, when bands of demons who roam the world find and grip you, shake you like the small, not very bright animal you actually are, and every one of those complex, almost miraculous liquids you hold deep within spills, as we say, down the leg?

well well

juicy wet vocables, the satisfaction to be found in I am about to greet you, a someone you are really waiting for, or maybe when you get mailed a check you did not expect, or the way you feel when you look down to the bottom of the well you have dug and see fresh water beginning to gather, that is well, though not yet gush, is more a spring doing what a spring does rather well when it works overtime as both noun and verb, not boiling but rising, finding a seam, water on the level, the level going up, folding and unfolding on itself. The entry says next to see *vulva*.

gulf

let us to Greece then, to *kolpos*, nothing but mother's bosom, the land
  alone, not a combo, not a mother-land, but first a mother then a land,
  under which you might find the *Alfeiós* stream rushing down a fissure
  and flowing into the sea-vault, where a new verb overtakes it, vaults it
  as it were, lunges at you like an eel, the gulf itself an enormous vault
  to keep treasure in, and fed by brook-water obeying the law of gravity,
  where water comes to rest, merging something sweet, abiding and
  brimming in us that wants to leave it alone, as in keep this vault
  locked.

oil

in the beginning was oil, abundance and overflow of the olive, earthen
  jars of it stored in caves or lodges where a fire is going, where you
  might breathe in cooking smoke, and hear the Armenian *ewi*, a sound
  that gives the tongue pleasure, a word-oil almost as good as the smell
  of meat on a spit, the fat dripping, blistering the flesh it lands on, the
  eager hand quick to grasp the *tekne* of liquids, that will gather oil
  into vats, stoke the fire, carve the runnels in stone parapets, that will
  tip vats on their spindles, pour hot oil down on the invaders looking
  up.

spill

to say it the right way you need to purse the lips in innocence, a trilling
daughter to teach you, her sippy cup, her giggle as we peek under the
blanket to see what she's hiding there, then add the sound of the sea-
swell we dive under together, the spill another name for a wave
cresting in thick crude, the feel of blunt trauma in the Saxon *spillan*,
rooted in blood slicks, the corpse-flowers in bloom, a white bit of
bone, a shred still stuck in the mace, that blunt, manly instrument
designed according to the rules of engagement, spill the word-father of
spoils.

drill

I will stop now this burrowing, though I would be derelict not to note
points of contact between the labor to bore holes in the earth face
and commands we use to move the platoon, that piercing call
to attention, the way we snap to, thumbs aligned on the trouser
seams, feet at a forty-five-degree angle, how we turn in unison, right
face, and lead off on the left foot, the boot-heel striking first, the
recruits in green waves of intact bodies flowing across the grinder,
that asphalt drill-field where the unit is tooled into a machine,
one more prone to mistakes but not unrelated to the spinning,
diamond-hard head of a deep water drill bit at the moment it breaks
through.

More or Less

I love the word *chthonic*.
Though when I say it, I feel as if I am talking
into a tin can, the string leading back to age nine.

The young self at the other end trusts me,
and promises not to pour the gasoline,
nor set the house on fire.

A good boy, he will grow up to read many
student essays, make abundant marginalia,
more or less about meaning.

Such self-splitting as this soup-can implies
has begun to worry me.
It's like waiting for the biopsy to come back.

The doctor on the phone is asking now if I *understand*.
I wonder silently to the ceiling,
how did the *that* he is talking about become the *me* I am?

I realize the question is only a feeling, more or less
a lens to view the subject through,
something to help bring the topic into focus.

I am starting to feel a bit lens-y and light sensitive myself.
I think I'll stay home today,
the plan being to dive under the duvet,

straight into my warm and singular scent.
If I sleep, I hope to go down into the murk,
walk the cave where stalagmites and stalactites

are trying to touch each other.
I'll find a dry spot where I can sit down, relax,
try not to worry. I will wait

to see what shows up, see what it has to say,
if there is anything to say,
more or less.

Delasanta

You at the desk in our early morning class,
Dante open before us, and some more misery
I ask you to explain, a labor that makes
you glow with the pleasure that comes
from showing the young how awful the real.

On doctrine we would no doubt disagree.
I was a khaki-and-loafers freshman learning
the intricacies of the medieval construct.
While sinners writhed, I tried to sort out
the day's given *contrapasso*, and you argued

their suffering was a sign of what moved
the spheres, what roused us each morning,
and brought me to our descent into hell,
and you to the wooden riser you taught from,
a bit of monastic on-high the Dominicans

kept in the classroom to help us see beauty
in the suicide's words oozing like sap from
the twigs snapped from the trees in which
Harpies roosted. You said here we could
glimpse the stern harmonic that governed.

I thought the calculus of the deity appalling,
but you were the stoic Roman, and I was
the shaken, muted Florentine. You labored
to reassure us, saying *the path upward
went down this way first, this way for us all.*

You, who bore lightly the name of everything holy.

Said Not Said

The Teacher

They bring before him a *woman taken in
adultery.* He is asked what is to be done,
for by law her head should be crushed by
stones. Trick question, writes the evangelist.
A ragged boy, watching from behind backs,
senses danger, while the Teacher ignores
the question utterly, *as if he heard them not.*
The boy squeezes front to see the Teacher
bend down, and with his finger, push aside
the sand, waiting for someone to pick up
the first stone. The book says nothing as
to what the Teacher wrote in the sand, or if
this was writing at all. Like the boy staring
at what look like chicken scratches, we are
left to wonder at the spell the unsaid casts
over them all. We feel unrelenting sunlight
bearing down on the accusers. We may try
to imagine what they are thinking but they,
convicted by their conscience, have begun
to walk away, and are saying nothing.

Chalk

Neat white sticks in cardboard packets,
worn nubs at the end of the school day,
the Sisters whose swirling habit sleeves
swept along the boards picking up dust.
When I was the lucky one to clean up,
I would bring erasers outside and clap
them against the walls, and each other.
Puffs of chalk-dust clouds would rise
through the trees, determined to leave.
The fine, powdery remains of words,
numbers, and solid geometric proofs,
complex sentences we diagrammed,
vertical line dividing subject and verb,
returned to limestone particles, silica,
remnants of shells, history in sediments,
our flimsy white truths, what I believed in.

In the Rapids

In the dream I sat down on the far edge
of the portico, out of the rain, and waited
for the doors to open. I read a poem with
the passing hope it would bring to mind
the voice of the one who now was gone.
The chapel doors parted, and our ushers
in white gloves handed out the program
printed on paper made to feel like vellum.
I took my place among the others, listened
as well as I could to the music and words
that flew like pigeons up to the rafters.
Then I too was upstairs standing in talk
that swirled around me like white water.
Elbows bumped into, the wine spilled on
skewered white plugs of scallop wrapped
in bacon. I shifted to be nearer the widow
who was standing alone in what sounded
like rapids roaring. I was proud I could
hold steady enough for anyone who might
need me. At the same time I felt an almost
overwhelming desire to apologize, although
to whom and for what, I just could not say.

Wet Gravel

Stone barrow on a point overlooking the sea,
a good place to take the last labored breath.
Quartz veins, shale, slate layers, the pressed
sandstone, thin lines we read the epochs in.
Rust and gray minerals down rivers in Zion.
A bit of brown miracle dirt from Chimayo.
The rock a boy threw at my head, the one
I pitched back at him. *Mickeys* we called them.
Cairns you see climbers build at the summit,
and mark the trail with on Kilauea caldera.
Glacial stones that migrate under the earth,
or sit as unmoved as the Buddha, hard enough
to break tines off a backhoe. Prayer-stones
we place with care and words atop the grave.
A white pebble at the bottom of Frost's well.
O stone, wrote Nguyễn Duy, thinking of lives
lost near Angkor. O bloodstones of Mycenae
that we sit on while we drink from our water.
The backyard stones a child will hammer open
to find the unequivocal silence inside of things.
Wet gravel paths we turn and face each other on.

Pear Tree in Flower

Sometimes a tree will do anything you ask.
You must speak to it softly, as carefully as you . . .

I am not kidding.

FOUR

The Left Hand

clay votive offering

Etruria, 3rd century BCE

maybe three inches tall

forget the museum's numbers on the wrist

look hard into the open palm instead

take your time

Body Body

That I was I knew was of my body, and what I should be I knew I should be of my body.
—Walt Whitman

In my opened, bare-assed johnny I am meeting up again
with you my aging trunk, wayward traveling companion,

old trading buddy, fat winter sleeping bag I carry with me
into my dreams, you my ne'er-do-well pardner on a mule

crossing the desert, old guy who keeps asking for a swig,
who soaks the sheets with worry, turns on me regularly,

remains hard to fathom, easy to ignore, impossible to trust,
years since we met, when first I cut in, and asked for a kiss.

Meltemi

A furious red clay dust should play a part,
and a wren too, the vocal frightened one,
so too whitecaps and the concrete blocks
with arms angled to make the water break.
Bring in a dog tethered to its birthplace,
and a boy in neck chain, who with a purple
ballpoint writes up the rental, and marks
with his highlighter the safer slab pull-offs.
Assemble the caves in the gorge, a gouge
in the walls, cold springs, the white chapel,
a candle burning under the blood-red glass.
Let massed winds from the north pour over
the groves that shudder, limbs that give up,
the gods everywhere, some you believe in.

The Migrants

He hid the fire in a tall hollow stalk of fennel,
out of the sight of the great one who delights in thunder.

—Hesiod

In those mountains he met others walking in the same direction. Backpacks, black plastic garbage bags, food sacks, a girl with two hard-boiled eggs, the shells flaking off. Some wore T-shirts from the sports teams of the West, and one man still carried an orange life jacket. The hunted, wayward god stood beside a mother who held her infant before her the same way he held the stalk that carried the embers he had stolen. He noted dry myrtle along the side of the road, and saw a ground that seemed soft enough for them to sleep on. There would be at least this much tonight, twigs for a fire, perhaps water for tea, some warmth in the morning.

Glad Day

Glad Day, and we are kneeling on a rise
    in the prairie, your arm resting on Albion,

the terrier we named after Blake's idea
    of what we all were before the Fall,

Glad Day that etched figure of innocence,
    sunburst of youth, radiant body, wide-armed,

his feet touching the sloping blue earth,
    Glad Day a face turning into pure light,

his limbs in a dance we hoped would last
    as long as we breathed, as long as this

Glad Day could hold in his extended fingers
    the warm browns of the prairie,

the blue vastness of sky, a dog in your arms,
    me with a lens, you looking back.

O Be

Driftwood logs,
the base of a waterfall as it empties,
water or time no matter,
a steady emanation, the inanimate
indifferent as ever to the pain
of a woman beyond weeping,
her fingers scratching the veins
along the back of her hand.
Where did I first see them,
these hands that slip back into the mist
and fall as far away as they can
from the bridge I stand on?
This worse than precarious spot,
the foam gathering under it,
giving in to whatever happens.
There are places designed for leaping,
heights so eager to please that the idea
of salvation was invented
to name the distance from here
to where the water pours into sunlight,
the sight of which turns me
into a sparrow clinging to a branch,
bead-eyes missing nothing,
wanting nothing more than this.

Call to Prayer

It begins in what one imagines as desert but is nothing empty.
For a second or two the air hints at the night it has risen from.

Then the call passes from voice to voice, saying *this is yours,*
take it on to the next, as if these words were waves in a storm,

each gaining on the other, growing stronger when they touch,
the song overtaking dawn at the rim of the valley just before

the words enter the old city by the gates of reason, finding
the byways piled high with what no one believes in anymore.

Stray cats, arching their backs when they hear it, cry out in pain.
We throw open the green metal shutters, and try to listen again.

Ecce

In his *Itinerary to the Sepulcher*, Petrarch's guide to the Holy Land,
      he declines to accompany a friend on pilgrimage.

The poet says he is not afraid of the journey, but prefers to map
      the way there in words.

He writes we *sometimes know many things we have never seen,*
      and many things that we have seen we do not know.

With this he sails his friend down the boot, crosses him to Messenia,
      to the Crusader citadels of *Methon and Coron,*

these and the other places he has only read about, but where, as he says,
      the sea washes on the way to Jerusalem.

—

Morning on the subway platform, melt-water seeping in from the
      unplowed, snowy streets.

White streaks on the tunnel walls bring to mind a man's jaw gripped
      by someone else's hand.

We know *many things we have never seen,* and I've read we praise God
      to prove to ourselves that God exists.

The face under a green terry-cloth towel cannot turn away from the hose
      or the water pouring out.

Under the clamor of the train coming in I see a mouse running toward its
    hole, desperate, I imagine, to be with its own kind.

—

In the Church of the Holy Sepulcher I felt a long invisible line pass
    through me.

I saw it rise from a stone field and pass on to milking cows, run through
    swollen fingers, brass thimbles, a wooden darning egg,

and bring me to the foot-worn paths of the city, to walk with pilgrims
    through the echoing rotunda,

a guide tapping his staff on the flagstone floor, pointing this way down
    to the tomb.

The *many things that we have seen* and *do not know.*

Out on the plaza when I left, I passed a Coptic priest squatting
    by a charcoal fire, the heat-treasure in winter.

I remember most the prayer he sang in a low, wavering voice,
    a song like a light snow trying not to fall.

Fennel

The soul, yes, was murky / and no one could see it.
                                    —Adélia Prado

Something of the fog has burned off—
something in the high oaks and behind
the sounds of hammers, ignitions—
a shift outward, a quick long view,
to a sliver of the largest bay there is.

A morning of pinion and stridor.

Of course, you were not one who
was for the high air and only remote.
You were for the light on the table,
the red gate that needed to be shut,
the irritable dog that hears the world

too much, the scruffy fledgling robin
that lands on the trellis, sizes me up
in the way of its kind, and decides
I am all right, just more evidence
of oddity found among the breathing.

At the end maybe you were thinking
of Whitman and his claim that dying
was luckier than we had supposed.
Or not. *Or not.* Here is the bee
that hovers over a newly fallen leaf.

How lovely the flower I do not know,
and where do I enter?

I remember cresting the ancient hill
at Dunkineely, seeing a blue caravan
in the pasture corner and thinking this
is all I will ever know of the soul,
the grass uncut, a land arm stretching

out to the south. I touch it again here
in the braille of small yellow blooms
I rub between my fingers, pass under
my nose, while a snail, with its horns
of light, works its way down the stem.

Olive Harvest

It's true, the tree has the scent of the sea,
        but the silver leaves, their slender fingers,

the thick, infinitely twined trunk, some riddle
        in the roots that lets it drink from the stones,

even the place where a limb has broken or
        been lopped off, the shoot that springs back

to life, stumps that burn for hour upon hour,
        a scattered discard twig you press to your lips,

and the fruit that hangs from young branches
        and old, a green reddening to black, this fruit

ripened on enough bloodshed and hardened
        human behavior to make you think it will turn

away in disgust, year after suffering year
        comes back, as if to say *here & here & here*

Fresh Ink

The museum like a dream, the dreams later
like the museum: dragons in trees, in clouds,
in the cornices, under an open-air platform
where five scholars read and collate the texts
messengers on horseback have brought back,
the scrolls unwound by servants whose brows
painted white declare the purity in their work.
The horses are weary, unfettered, calmer than
the sages who bend down and read, read again,
and pass the text on perhaps with a new line
added to a poem in fresh ink—a sweet, dark,
and slightly metallic smell—ink like a purple
flower that opens only in the summer night.
Attendants in the dream support with extended
arms the length of the scroll, an ache on behalf
of the need to save, the scholar's desire to set
in place what will be needed, insisting history
comes to us from the provinces tied in bundles
like the sheaves of grain from a half-tilled field
visible in the distance, where the workers rest,
among them a pair of lovers asleep in high sun,
their limbs entwined enough for them to know
they are together even in this dream where I see
under the pavilion a painter whose gaze takes in
the whole story from beginning to end and now
must decide which line before him is an eyelash,
and which, merely the trembling of his hand.

Sixteen

the soul / struggling to become your soul
                    —George Seferis

1

at the far end of a sacred road—a grove of ruins for the rich

2

this heavy air—a night that promises only the mosquitoes

3

some poems I never much understand—I think this reason enough

4

from now on become what I behold—the orange, stem and leaf

5

steps out fresh from my shower—a woman I've never seen before

6

an inflatable raft with two kids on—the father churning the bay

7

high and barely visible, two fighter jets—ours and not ours

8

bougainvillea—what maiden fled from a god to become you

9

surprise for my mother and father and me too—good flesh failing

10

my love has fallen back to swaddling sleep—I will go there too

11

pity the poor blue cicada flat on its back—with a song and without

12

cliff swallows wheel and dart—tending to matters of their state

13

I love the broken unfinished sentence—I love my own angry—

14

inside the quarried stone—you see the mason and his silver chisel

15

I had to go a long way to find the cypress tree—I was born under

16

toting up money—dividing it by the years I have left—*this many*

The Day Later

On the bridges my tires drum out a meter—
too late, too little, *The Separate*
      Notebooks not enough,
admit it—you are still a schoolboy,
slate in hand, *your only theme was time—*

its questions coming in on sunlight that lands
on two flea-market trinkets—a bronze
      dog, a milky swallow,
one from your mother, the other
from mine—it is early evening and I still

don't understand how to think about the dead—
the poised Saint Bernard ready
      to dig someone out,
the glass swallow soaring down
as if the earth had more to offer than air.

I am glad to find them again, grateful
they are still with me, and in this
      they are like the sparrow
outside my window pecking at insects
in the gutter, tapping out what could be words

in a long sentence on the verge of forming,
and I think *of all I have not said—*
      the dry saw grass by
Bodega Bay, the pastured cows
trying to figure out what possible harm or good

Edwin my teacher and I meant as we walked
without talking about the war
          I thought I should go to—
Now he sits, poet at the window, saying
he loves the alder leaves, how they stay still

yet change and fall away like memory.
In the film he tells us to remember how
          to forget, no more—
The idea rises from the center of being,
and points at what his words alone cannot say,

what you hear when the car turns into the drive,
and the front door opens on
          a house gone dark,
the day later, and a person you love calls
up the attic stairs, wondering if you are home.

shade laurel

scent of sage and thyme

a brown goat that turns back to stare

what took you so long?

Notes

Psalm
The poem ends on the first line of the fourth Psalm. Translation is from *The New Jerusalem Bible*.

The Unacceptable
For Mary Patricia Brown (1931–2009).

Cement Mixer
Refers to a song composed by Bulee "Slim" Gaillard (1916–1991), an American jazz singer and virtuoso pianist, author of several such "novelty songs."

The Name of the Painting
Titian's *The Rape of Europa* (c. 1650) is in Boston's Isabella Stuart Gardner Museum.

Here is what the mind does
The poem is for Juliano Mer Khamis (1958–2011), founder of the Freedom Theatre in Jenin. The title of the poem is from "Untitled," a poem by Karl Kirchwey in his *At the Palace of Jove* (2002).

Marwan,
The Arabic قسوة translates into harshness bordering on cruelty. The English phonetic pronunciation is *qusweh*.

Quảng Tri Elegy
The title refers to the northernmost province of what was called South Vietnam during the years of the American war. The poem is dedicated to Kevin Bowen and Nguyễn Bá Chung.

The Peach
Võ Quê is a poet, musician, and singer from Huế, Việt Nam.

Crossing Nguyễn Du Street

Nguyễn Du (1766–1820) is the author of the Vietnamese epic poem *The Tale of Kiều*.

Passage Tomb

For John F. Deane. The passage tomb referred to is at Knowth, in the Boyne Valley, Co. Meath, Ireland.

Ghost Ranch

The title refers to the New Mexico ranch where Georgia O'Keeffe often worked and where she did the 1935 painting *Ram's Head, White Hollyhock-Hills*. The epigraph is from a letter by O'Keeffe to the photographer Anita Pollitzer.

Wod-or

For Nick Flynn, and in response to the Deepwater Horizon oil spill. Literal elements in these etymologies are based on entries in the *Online Etymology Dictionary* and *The American Heritage Dictionary*.

Delasanta

For Rodney Delasanta (1932–2007).

Said Not Said

The story of the woman taken in adultery and the writing in the sand is told in the Gospel of John. The italicized lines belong to the evangelist.

Pear Tree in Flower

For Maxine and Earll Kingston.

The Left Hand

This clay votive offering is in the Gregorian Etruscan Museum in the Vatican, and its image is used with permission. I first encountered a photograph of this hand in "Healer Cults and Sanctuaries," an entry in *Antiqua Medicina: From Homer to Vesalius*, an online exhibit prepared by the Historical Collections and Services at the University of Virginia.

Body Body

The epigraph is from "Crossing Brooklyn Ferry."

Meltemi

The title refers to the north-south summer gales on the Aegean.

The Migrants

For Jean Valentine. The epigraph paraphrases lines in Richmond Lattimore's translation of Hesiod's *Works and Days*.

Ecce

The italicized lines are from Petrarch's epistolary poem *Guide to the Holy Land: Itinerary to the Sepulcher of Our Lord Jesus Christ* (1358), translated by Theodore J. Cachey.

Fennel

For Seamus Heaney (1939–2013). The epigraph is from Prado's poem "The Transfer of the Body," translated by Ellen Doré Watson.

Olive Harvest

For the Interfaith Peace Builders organization, and its ongoing delegations to Israel and Palestine.

Fresh Ink

The poem refers to a Chinese horizontal scroll painting, *Northern Qi Scholars Collating Classical Texts*, attributed to Yan Liben (c. 600–673). It is in the Museum of Fine Arts in Boston and was part of a 2010 exhibition titled *Fresh Ink*.

Sixteen

The epigraph is from Seferis's poem "Mycenae," translated by Edmund Keeley and Philip Sherrard.

The Day Later

For Edwin Honig (1919–2011). The italicized lines are from "The Separate Notebooks: A Mirrored Gallery" by Czesław Miłosz. These lines translated by Robert Hass and Renata Gorczynska. The film referred to is *First Cousin Once Removed*, a 2012 documentary by Alan Berliner about Honig.

Acknowledgments

Heartfelt thanks to the editors of the following journals for publishing many of the poems in this book, some in earlier versions and with different titles.

AGNI, Barrow Street, Beloit Poetry Journal, Button, Consequence, Field, Gulf Coast, Harvard Review, The Massachusetts Review, The Ocean State Review, Plume, Poetry International, Post Road, Providence College Magazine, Salamander, Sanctuary (New England Audubon Society), *Solstice, spoKe, Taos Journal of Poetry and Art.*

Equally heartfelt thanks go out to the editors who included these poems in the following anthologies.

A Ritual to Read Together (Woodley Press): "Call to Prayer"
Lay Bare the Canvas (The Loft Anthology): "The Name of the Painting"
So Little Time (Green Writers Press): *"shade laurel"*

I am very grateful for a residency at the Heinrich Böll Cottage on Achill Island, Co. Mayo, Ireland, where I began several of the poems in this book. I also want to thank the writers I have taught and learned from in various workshop settings over the past few years: the Bay Area Veteran Writers Group, the Boston Warrior Writers, the Colrain Poetry Manuscript Conference, the Fine Arts Work Center in Provincetown, the Robert Frost House, the Hudson Valley Writers' Center, the Suffolk University Creative Writing Program, and the William Joiner Institute for the Study of War and Social Consequences at UMass–Boston.

For advice and myriad forms of help as this book was being written, I also want to thank Bernard Avishai, Kevin Bowen, Francesco Buranelli, John F. Deane, Nir Eisikovits, David Ferry, Nick Flynn, Joan Houlihan, Ken Greenberg, Stratis Haviaras, Earll Kingston, Maxine Hong Kingston,

Glen Moriwaki, Nguyễn Bá Chung, Bob Scanlan, Lee Sharkey, Len Sommer, Kim Stafford, Pat Steenland, Jean Valentine, Helen Vendler, Võ Quê, Afaa Michael Weaver, and Kaethe Weingarten.

A special word of thanks as well goes out to William Corbett for his insight and sense of what artwork might grace the cover, and to Peter Sacks for creating an image that looks and feels so exactly right.

I especially want to acknowledge and thank Jennifer Barber, James Carroll, Martha Collins, George Kalogeris, and David Rivard for reading the earliest as well as later drafts of this book. A deep bow of gratitude goes out to everyone at Graywolf Press, especially to Caroline Nitz, Susannah Sharpless, Marisa Atkinson, Katie Dublinski, Jeff Shotts, and Fiona McCrae. Finally, all that has been said and not said in these poems simply would not be were it not for Stefi Gail Rubin.

FRED MARCHANT is the author of four previous books of poetry, including *Full Moon Boat* and *The Looking House*. His first book, *Tipping Point*, won the 1993 Washington Prize from the Word Works, and was recently reissued in a twentieth-anniversary second edition. *House on Water, House in Air*, a new and selected poems, was published in Ireland. He is the editor of *Another World Instead*, a selection of William Stafford's early poetry. With Nguyễn Bá Chung, he has co-translated *From a Corner of My Yard*, poems by Trần Dăng Khoa, and *Côn Đảo Prison Songs*, poems by Võ Quê, both published in Hà Nội. Emeritus Professor of English at Suffolk University in Boston, Marchant is the founding director of that school's creative writing program and its Poetry Center. He lives in Arlington, Massachusetts.

The text of *Said Not Said* is set in ITC Giovanni Book. Book design by Rachel Holscher. Composition by Bookmobile Design and Digital Publisher Services, Minneapolis, Minnesota. Manufactured by Thomson Reuters on acid-free, 30 percent postconsumer wastepaper.